Paul

with Best Wishes

from MIRZA Kazim

21/07/2016

To My Amma

WORLD'S ECHO

Zainab Kazim

ISBN 1-872460-00-3

Front cover by
Eqbal Mehdi

First Edition September 1989
Second Edition July 1992

Printed and Published in Great Britain by
Star Printers and Publishers (U.K.) Limited
33 Weatherby Road
Luton, LU4 8QS, England
Tel: Luton (0582) 581572

A Few Words of Thanks

"Praise be to Allah, Lord of all Worlds,
The Beneficient, the Merciful"

I would like to thank my parents under whose guidance I discovered the desire to learn and then to begin writing myself. It is their love, and their sacrifices that have brought me to this level. No words, no poetry – absolutely nothing – can express the way I feel about them.

I would like to thank Uncle Ashoor for encouraging me to write more and for showing great interest in my work.

My sincere thanks are also due to Uncle Kalbe Sadiq, who with deep affection appreciated my work more than I deserved. His kind attitude has forced me to attempt to bring myself to the standard of his appreciation.

I would like to thank my English teacher, Miss Plews, for kindly agreeing to write her comments on my work and correcting the punctuation in a large number of my poems. I am equally indebted to Mrs. Thakoordin for giving up her valuable time to advise me and write her comments on my poetry.

I would also like to thank Uncle Usmani for writing his comments on my poems and for boosting me with his infectious enthusiasm.

Thanks also to Roohi Baji who gave me her father's poetry book which influenced and improved my technique. I also thank her for her advice and for correcting many of my poems.

And last but certainly not least, I would again like to thank my family for all their effort without which this book would certainly not have been possible.

Zainab Kazim

Contents

SECTION III

SECTION IV

What They Think:

1. Miss Elizabeth J. Plews, B.A.
   Senior Teacher
   Head of English Department
   Challney Girls High School
   Stoneygate Road, Luton LU4 9TJ

2. Mrs. Doreen Thakoordin, B.A.
   Co-ordinator of Multicultural Education
   Challney Boys High School
   Stoneygate Road, Luton LU4 9TJ

3. Mr. Fazlur R. Usmani, B.A., M.A.
   London

4. Dr. Syed Kalbe Sadiq
   Lucknow, India

I have known Zainab since she joined the school and have had the pleasure of teaching her for some of that time. She has made very good progress in her studies and always shows a keen, interested attitude to learning. This year she has shown a sensitive response to literature, and this was emphasised to me when she asked that I look at some poems which she had written herself. I was surprised by the range of the poetry and the depth of her knowledge; the poems develop both in content and style. She obviously has an appreciation of the world about her and particularly of historical events and contemporary issues. Considerable emotion is contained within the subject matter; a response that is admirable in one so young, showing wisdom and maturity beyond her years. At present she has adopted the rhyming couplet as her particular style, which suits the narrative she wishes to express. Her range of vocabulary is wide, and she has used some vivid images and figures of speech. I hope to see her experimenting further with the actual skills of poetry.

I was honoured to be asked both to read Zainab's work and to write this preface. I am sure that such a dedicated young lady will go from strength to strength, and I look forward to her future successes, which she will certainly achieve.

Elizabeth J. Plews

I am very pleased to be invited to introduce the reader to this most interesting anthology.

One can detect, as one examines the collection from a chronological standpoint, the poet's growing maturity – from the somewhat forced rhymes and strained metre characteristic of everyone's first poetic efforts to the effective economy of language and abandonment of regular metre and rhyme indicative of the later work. What a wonderful milestone it is in every young poet's life when one realises that half-rhyme or blank verse can 'work', and that one can organise one's metre freely to achieve effect! When that happens, the realisation dawns that a poem is truly the expression of the poet's experience in which the reader is privileged to share. Zainab has made, at least in part, that discovery, and the future bodes well both for the poet herself and her readers.

What is also encouraging to me is the range of subject-matter, style and length. Here is a young lady who has firm views about the ways in which our world is organised and ruled and conducts its affairs, and states those opinions boldly: juxtaposed with these 'strong' poems are touching personal tributes to her grandmother and her brother, for example. Zainab's descriptive poems are among the most evocative in the collection, and her religious poetry is at once instructive and moving.

Here, then, is an anthology by a poet who can only grow in strength and commitment. If Zainab's work can be characterised by such powerful ideas and imagery at sixteen, who can guess what brilliance she will be able to achieve in later years?

That is for the future: for the present, I urge the reader to read and enjoy this marvellous first anthology, which I thoroughly recommend.

Doreen Thakoordin

Zainab Kazim is the lover of mankind and the friend of friends. She is either mentally millions of miles away or else dissecting you under an invisible microscope. Poems like "Blacks of Africa", "Ethiopia" and "Hiroshima and Nagasaki" are the manifestations of these natural and acquired attributes, where the world is lying like a patient in front of her and Zainab is busy cutting it into parts for the simple purpose of minute examination.

You will have to be constantly prepared for the unexpected with Zainab. She is kind and tranquil by nature. She is courteous and soft-spoken simultaneously. She can be most amazing at the most unpredictable times.

Zainab is born and brought up by nature, to her the "meanest flower that blows can give thoughts too deep for tears". Nature is her master, guide and rule. She is also like a child amidst the marvels of nature and she cries like a child after beholding each and every natural phenomenon.

"The sky grows dark, the wind grows cold.
Everywhere the mist unfolds."

Zainab belongs to everyone and yet to no one, hence her collection of poems are varied and many. They refer to past, present and future, here and hereafter. I find Zainab's collection of poems interesting reading, light-bearing and fruit-bearing.

A glance over many and perusal of some of the poems of the young lady Zainab Kazim aged 15 is a treat for the mind and vision. It diverts one's imagination to many of the happenings of the past as well as the present.

It is really amazing that at this tender age Zainab can feel human sufferings so deeply and reflect her impressions so effectively in her poems. The couplet:

"Long ago my beloved died"
I wait to be buried by his side"

in the poem "Nobody Cares" shows how vividly little Zainab thinks of serious eventualities of life. Similarly her poems "The Blacks of Africa will be Free" and "Hiroshima and Nagasaki" indicate sublime dimensions of her thought which could hardly be expected from a young girl.

The question she poses in the couplet:

"Children are born and as children they die
I ask myself O why? O why?"

is a question that may occur to many developing minds. This is a natural thought and has a positive answer from the Islamic point of view. The concluding couplet in the poem "Noah's Ark" reflects the Divine will in the following words:

"Noah's work was finally done
He had destroyed the sinners – everyone."

Similarly the first encounter of Imman Husain with Hur and the sublime human behaviour of the Imam sets the stage for a change of mind on the part of Hur in the line:

"Goodbye Hur, we will meet again."

In her poem "Saqqa-e-Sakina" (The Water Carrier of Sakina) many of her couplets fill the eyes of the reader with tears especially when she mentions the horse who refuses to drink prior to its master. The passionate request of Imam Husain to Abbas to address him as brother when Abbas' soul was about to depart is most effectively portrayed by this young angel named Zainab Kazim. God bless this pride of our Islamic heritage.

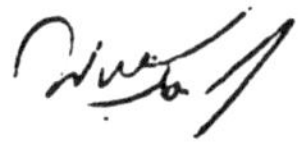

A PRAYER

My Lord, You made the gentle breeze,
The laughing flowers, the noble trees,

The flowing rivers, the trickling streams,
The massive great rocks that pull from the seams,

And you created man an intelligent being,
But death and sorrow he tries to bring.

You gave him food – but he wastes that too,
Instead of feeding the hungry few.

He burns it in the fields and sinks it in the sea,
He wastes and wastes and wastes for economy.

You created man to live in peace,
But there are wars that do not cease.

You created man equal – black, brown or white,
But racism is strong in every right.

You created this beautiful world for man alone,
But with nuclear weapons he destroys his home.

See how wasteful man has become,
You gave him the chance to choose right from wrong.

But he has chosen the evil path,
Soon he will taste Your anger and wrath.

My Lord have mercy upon Mankind,
Take away his evil mind.

Give him instead a tender heart,
That he may joyfully with money part,

And feed the hungry and the poor,
And end for all time, the scourge of war,

And treat his fellow men the same,
And from evil may he refrain.

My Lord, please make my dreams come true,
And keep me away from evil too.

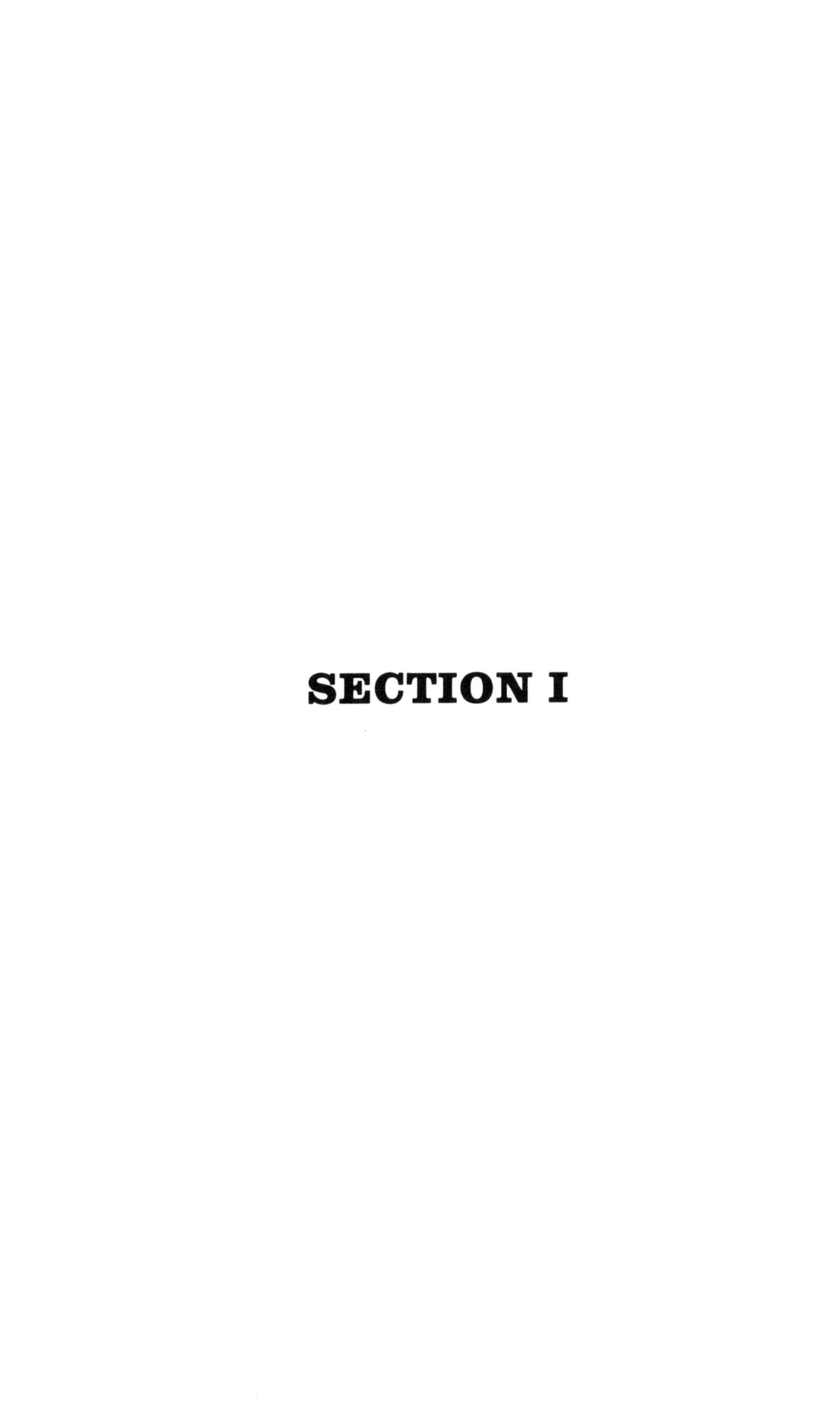

SECTION I

HIROSHIMA AND NAGASAKI

Long ago in the year 'forty five
When the war raged on and many died.

America and Japan were at war,
As they had been for years before.

America ordered Japan to give in,
But Japan was proud and wouldn't do this thing.

America threatened, with a bomb this time,
And she was willing to commit this crime.

Japan refused, just like before,
So America ended 'The Second World War'.

She sent a plane to bomb Japan,
The destruction of many a noble man.

It floated over, like a shadow of doom,
It dropped two bombs, and two cities went 'BOOM'.

Screams of terror filled the sky,
As many were painfully burnt alive.

The flames rose higher and higher still,
As many were sadly and horribly killed.

Children wandered through the streets, alone,
Trying to find a burnt out home.

But all they found were the wounded or dead,
What sad thoughts must have filled their heads.

Japan surrendered very soon,
For her it was a time of gloom.

The Japanese were filled with utter shame,
Many felt they could never see the world again.

Many think America was right
By bombing Japan and ending this fight.

But they do not see how many died,
Or how many people were burnt alive,

Or how many were crippled for their life span,
It was a fatal wound on the soul of Japan,

O Mankind! Hope with me,
Pray there is no 'World War Three'!

THE UNITED NATIONS

During World War II in 1945,
When homes were wrecked and many died,

Several countries got together,
To defeat the axis powers forever.

These countries still remain –
They are still the very same.

They SAY that they struggle for peace,
They SAY they want the wars to cease.

For this peace they bombed Japan,
For this peace they fought Iran,

For this peace Libya was bombed,
And many innocent people were wronged.

Is this the peace that they desire?
Or are these the wars they will acquire?

Not all the countries bear the guilt,
Only five bear the guilt.

Five rich countries who decide
Who should be bombed and who should survive.

If just one of these countries disagrees,
The plans will automatically cease.

That one country will have her way,
None of the others will have a say.

These five countries are powerful and strong,
They think might is right, but it is wrong.

Theirs is a very backward way,
Countries bear what they do and say.

Come now let us join as one,
And destroy these evils – everyone.

THE BLACKS OF AFRICA WILL BE FREE

When black Africa was a free free land
Black tribes roamed her golden sand.

They worked hard, and stayed alive,
Men and women side by side.

They were happy and wanted no more,
But for them there was misery in store.

One dark night when the moon had gone,
And only the fires blazed off and on,

A large ship came in to land
Upon Africa's savannah sand.

The white men had finally come,
They came to enslave the strong and young.

The blacks were whipped and tortured too,
Their hopelessness and misery only grew.

They were taken to strange strange lands,
By whites with whips and powerful hands.

They were made to work to the point of pain;
They felt they would never be happy again.

Back in Africa, their long lost home,
The whites had murdered, robbed and grown.

The whites took over Africa too;
It was theirs now, the blacks knew.

The whites now rule the African land,
Apartheid has conquered her savannah sand.

The young blacks want to fight,
Fight for their freedom and their right.

They want the world to look and see,
The blacks of Africa will be FREE.

PALESTINE

Silence reigns in the sultry street,
No-one is seen in this baking heat.

Except for a youth, stone cold dead,
A bullet shot, through his lifeless head.

A stone held in his unmoving hand,
A pool of blood smearing the golden sand.

The earth is hot with sadness and dread,
Stained dark with the blood of the dead.

This is Palestine's bloodstained sand,
This, my friends, is the Promised Land.

This unrest in Palestine began long ago,
The roots of this, you ought to know.

In Europe the Jews had a troublesome stay,
The Europeans liked not their religion and ways.

And when there occurred a fearsome war,
The allied powers conquered more and more.

They defeated the Turkish Empire as well,
The world became a pit of hell.

In the Balfour Declaration, the British gave
Palestine away,
For the Jews as their homeland for them to stay.

But there for centuries, Muslims had lived in peace,
With Christians and Jews, there had only been
peace.

And only now, recently so,
The Jews have claimed it for their own.

Muslim villages have been wiped away,
Jewish towns have come in their place.

Millions of Muslims have fled the land,
The Jews have taken the Palestinian sand.

Moses promised it to them as the Promised Land,
So that they could live in peace upon its sand.

He wanted them to live in peace,
But there is a war that does not cease.

Some Arab Palestinians refuse to go,
This is the only land they know.

Their villages have been wiped away,
Jewish towns have come in their place.

Day by day their frustration grows,
At Israeli soldiers they can only throw stones.

These Arab Palestinians are willing to die,
With bullets the Jewish Israeli soldiers reply.

Back in the humid Palestinian street,
A broken hearted mother weeps.

Over the body of her only son,
Of the many victims – he was one.

For his homeland he did fight,
He fought for his land and his right.

His blood drenched body lies upon the sand,
The stone lies limp in his unmoving hand.

The sky holds back its tears no more,
Its tear drops cry at this bloody war.

And the shrieking wind seems to whine,
"Don't destroy yourself, O Palestine!

O Jews of Palestine try to understand,
Would Moses want bloodshed upon his Holy Land?"

A MESSAGE TO BRITAIN FROM AN ARAB PALESTINIAN

You gave the Jews my Palestine,
Yet Palestine is my people's and mine.

The Jews try to take my land,
Millions of my people flee its sand.

The Jews shoot women and children too,
O Britain this is because of you.

Palestine O Britain is my people's and mine,
You gave the Jews my Palestine.

Yet, O Britain, you SIT drinking tea,
YOU could not care about my people and me.

It is not you who must see children shot in the head,
Or men and women wounded and dead.

O Britain! O Britain! Look and see,
See what you have done to my people and me.

THE STORM

Like erupting black rocks they gather overhead,
Freezing my frightened brain with dread,
Spitting ice bullets in my wake,
Numbing my limbs until they ache.
Heartless winds around me blow,
Pushing me where I want not to go.
Like cannons they boom and suffocate my plea,
Living,
I die,
For I am not free.

SHATILA AND SABIRA

In a lonely camp, a silent place,
Death leers its ugly face.

It pokes its' sneer into every vent,
Blood and sorrow is it's lament.

Everywhere there are bodies of the dead,
Around them are pools of thick dark red.

There are bullet holes everywhere,
Careless bullets fired here and there.

In men and women, children as well,
Each bullet has a cruel story to tell.

Nothing moves. It's silent and still.
The camp is silent, so quiet and still.

But over there! A boy raises his head,
He looks around at the bodies of the dead.

The Israeli soldiers have all gone,
He gets up and walks along.

Looking at everything everywhere,
Isn't there life anywhere?

As he walks on the tears sting his eyes,
It is then he hears lamenting cries.

Someone's alive, at last, at last!
He rushes to the place very fast.

There are people still alive,
He is not the only one to survive.

This event happened in the year 'eighty four,
Many were killed – ten thousand or more.

For twenty-four hours the firing went on.
Till thousands of people were dead and gone.

The survivors were very very few,
They tried to build their camps anew.

But only three years later they were intimidated
again,
This time by the Militia men.

They prevented food from getting in,
A vile and vindictive inhumane sin.

For often in those camps children were seen,
Trying to get some food in.

Rarely these children did return,
Mostly in their backs the bullets would burn.

And the silent world watched on.
As the destruction of these camps went on and on . . .

ETHIOPIA

Around the world thousands die,
Their lives go painfully passing by.

Their bones stick out from beneath their skin;
Their stomachs grumble from deep within.

Their hearts are weak, but their spirits are high,
They depend on others for their food supply.

Some send them food and water too –
All packed and parcelled – good as new.

Their camps are filled with dead and woe,
Their number of dead continue to grow.

Children are born, and as children they die,
I ask myself "O why? O why?"

A mother holds her ailing child,
Its starved face is pure and mild.

She leaves the child upon the sands,
The babe clutches her bony hands.

Tenderly she holds the infant away,
Then takes the bowl and is on her way.

Soon she returns with a bowl of food,
It's warming and filling and looks so good.

The baby is silent – it does not speak.
Its eyes are closed, and it looks so weak.

She lets out a sob and holds her head,
"My child is dead!
My child is dead . . . "

OUR BRITISH NATIONAL HERITAGE

What jolly good fun we had, old chap,
Eating treasures from India's own sack.

Awfully jolly horrendous heat around, but
Remember those jolly jewels we found?
Easily they were a jolly exceptional find,

Though we could have jolly well left them all behind.
Had such jolly good fun digging up the Pharoah's jolly tomb,
Ingots of gold, precious plates, and jolly spoons,
Easily made a bloody jolly billion in that trip,
Verbally gave those jolly Egyptians the slip,
Enterprisingly brought our jolly treasures back home,
So that as British heritage they can jolly well be known.

IRON LADY

An iron head
Swivels round
To glare across
An iron domain.
Cold blue eyes watch
Cautiously
Iron people
Working mechanically
To her commands.
All is well.
She is arrogant.
Proud.
Despising all that is
Non-iron.
She hates steel,
Copper,
Aluminium
And all else.
Except iron.
A china doll.
Enters her land.
She tears off her arms.
And legs
And sends her
Out of her domain.
An iron man
Sheds iron tears.
She ignores him.
He leaves her dominion.
Mumbling
To himself
Lest she overhears.
Her iron face smiles
Ruthlessly.
She is master of all,
Ruler of everything,
Queen of all she surveys.

PARTY POLITICAL BROADCAST

The window I watch through
Is of the most economical glass,
Even the trees have been planted economically,
For I have taken into consideration
That there is a rapidly rising demand
For trees,
Due to which inflation may arise.
This furniture also
Has been purchased
From a declining industry.
If there are too many disintegrations,
The country will dissipate.
How will we cope?
See these sofas, lampstands, bookcases –
They have not been bought for my comfort,
But for the good of our country.
Vehemently
And unvehemently
I disapprove
And approve
Of declining countries
My conscientious
And hard working nature
Has been the cause of my success.
And from my present state of success,
I will survive
To encompass further boundaries!
During the next two days
I will reduce inflation by fifty per cent,
Increase national output by seventy-five per cent,
And will totally and scrupulously
Wipe out all forms of crime!
Vote for me!
Vote for me!
Vote for me!

SECTION II

LONELINESS

Loneliness is an isolated boy
In a crowded room.
Whose eyes
Are not met.
Whose smile
Remains unanswered.
Whose only sound
Is an anguished cry
That comes from the heart.
Who tastes
Salt water
That quenches no thirst,
And that falls like dew.
Who feels knives,
Carving and creeping their way
Through his heart.

JEALOUSY

She pounces upon the neck.
Chewing and gnawing
The meat
Hungrily.
At first
There is resistance.
Then acknowledged defeat.
She is proud
Of her conquest
And arrogantly guards
The whimpering flesh.
No-one approaches:
So leaving the
Rotting carcass,
She slinks off
To find
A more challenging
Victim.

THE WAITING

The hospital is silent
And still
But for the impatient
Tap tap tap tap of a
Hand.
The sudden movement of the eye.
The tense wet hand,
Quenching in sorts,
A dripping forehead.
Quick excited
Glances at
A 'photo.
Fidgeting hands.
Tense shoulders
Jerking back with a start
At a sound.
The body heaves forward
To the door.
A cynical clinical smell.
Nobody.
A dense shattered sigh.
A bell rings.
The rush of a body to a door.
The door opens,
Slowly.
A person.
Ears lean forward.
. . . 'He's dead!' . . .

TICK TOCK

The watch ticks.
Tick tock.
Tick tock.
Hands move.
She waits.
Tick tock.
The station
Is secretive,
Silent.
Tick tock.
The sky weeps.
Tick tock.
He is not there.
Tick tock.
Nearly three.
Tick tock.
She falls
Onto the
Track.
Tick tock.
The train speeds in.
Tick tock.
Tick tock.
A man rushes
To the platform.
Tick tock.
Tick tock.
Tick tock.

NOBODY CARES

I sit alone in the upstairs room,
Staring into darkness and into gloom.

My eyes are weak, my ears can't hear,
I sit alone in endless fear.

My heart is sad and weak within,
My body is withered, and my face so grim.

I'm cold and lonely, sad and weak,
My present so sad – my future bleak.

Long ago, my beloved died,
I wait to be buried by his side.

AMBITIONS

I want to be Rudolf's red nose
On a cold winter's morning,
Or Santa's sledge
Sliding with prezzies
Across the snow,
Or the tiny warm fire
In the fireplace
Waiting . . .
To scorch Santa's bottom!

THE LAND OF DREAMS

When the clock strikes eight, and the land is dark,
Lights switch on like burning sparks.

Little children go to bed,
And fall asleep with a kiss on the head.

Then go off to the land of dreams,
Where there are gardens and bubbling streams.

And little gnomes that come alive,
And catch silver fishes that slither and slide.

And flowers begin to dance and sing,
Bringing together the beauty of spring.

I wonder if this is what the children dream,
When they go off to the 'Land of Dreams'.

HOME SWEET HOME

The sky grows dark, the wind grows cold,
Everywhere the mist unfolds.

Not a thing is seen on this dark night,
When every move fills you with fright.

Something moves – frightfully near,
A black cat does appear.

It walks before you, making you stop.
Something falls with a 'slop'.

It's raining hard, again, once more,
A night like this was never before.

You move faster, making haste –
In your mouth is a salty taste.

You're shivering now, but not from cold,
Over you fear takes hold.

Look! Look! Your home is near,
Gone now, is that shadow of fear.

Now you heave, a happy sigh,
Soon you'll be out of this winter's nigh'.

At last you've ended your lonely roam,
You've returned to your wonderful 'Home Sweet
Home'.

MOONLIGHT MAGIC

When the clock strikes twelve, and the moon is out,
The dolls in the dolls' house come quietly out.

The soldiers in the cupboard, the train on the floor,
The 'plane on the shelf, and the teddy by the door.

They go outside into the night,
And sing and dance in the moonlit night.

The teddy climbs up into the train,
The dolls clamber inside the 'plane.

Together they have a wonderful time,
Laughing and having a great old time.

But soon the sun climbs up high,
The day has come – it's no longer nigh'.

They all return to their places again,
And let the fresh young day begin.

SLEEP WELL

A seagull glides towards a setting sun,
Her day's work is nearly done.

She watches the sun sink into the waves,
The sea engulfing its burning rays.

An orange glow marks where it had been,
But the sun is now nowhere to be seen.

The bird feels sleepy, she needs a rest,
Slowly she glides towards her nest.

A black shadow soon covers the land,
Nothing is seen – not even the sand.

From behind the clouds comes the silvery moon,
It brightens the darkness and the gloom.

Its glow lights up the dull yellow sand,
And shines across the sleeping land.

On it glides throughout the night,
Bidding the sleepers, all 'Goodnight'.

SECTION III

MY AMMA

It seems like only yesterday,
So near and yet so far away.

When I sat silent by your side,
Loving and caring – watching mesmerized.

Gazing at your silver hair,
Your folded skin, so aged and fair.

Your sad, soft, brown, tear filled eyes,
That sad mouth that uttered those sighs.

It seems like only yesterday,
So near and yet so far away.

I remember you resting on your tidy bed,
Resting your aged, lonesome head.

Being tortured by your memories,
Sad, lost, cruel memories.

Your kind husband who died long ago,
Your baby daughter whom you hardly did know.

Your son who died before your eyes,
No wonder you uttered those shattered sighs.

And when the time for prayer would come,
You'd go to pray like everyone.

Each faltering step would be torture for you,
But your faith in God continuously grew.

Walking along with unseeing eyes,
Uttering again, those broken sighs.

With each step you'd utter a tiny prayer,
Old age is so cruel and unfair.

Not a complaint would you utter or say,
When you finally sat down to pray.

You'd lift your hand to the skies,
And look to God with your aged eyes.

Now that you are dead and gone,
I wonder of your grave all alone.

The grave to which I've never been,
In the empty wilderness where few are seen.

And when I look at the dull grey sky,
I wonder where in heaven you lie.

And if you can see me from up there,
I want you to know that I still care.

MEMORIES

Remember when you told me
You were going to spike your hair.
I thought you were joking.
But you weren't!
Can you remember how shocked
Everyone was?
"What have you done to your face?"
"You used to look cute."
"Meet my brother from America."
You thought it was funny.
I didn't.
I wanted to invent some
Hair-growing tonic
Or hide your hair
In a scarf.
Or tear off my own
And glue it on your head.

Remember when we were very young
And Bubba, Mimmi, you and I
Returned home
Exhausted and hungry.
And I went straight to bed.
Remember how you came up and fed me,
Equally tired.
Putting up with my complaints
Of waking me up
When I hadn't really
Gone to sleep.

Remember how once
Bubba and Mimmi didn't get back
Till late
And I started to cry.
Remember how you comforted me
And told me that
They would soon return.
And you took out
A book.
And we sat down
To read it together

And then how,
Like a miracle,
They returned.

So how can you remember
And laugh
When I say I want to find you
A lovely wife?
Or smile cheekily
When I say
"Work hard!"
Or tell how I feel
On those empty days
When I'm alone
And I kiss a photograph
Whispering
"Come back home. Come back home."

SECTION IV

NOAH'S ARK

Long ago, when tyrants ruled,
And people were mean and very cruel.

And the world was filled with evil and sin,
And had very little goodness within.

Then the Good Lord God, the Supreme Knower,
Created a man, by the name of Noah.

Noah wasn't like the other men,
They were evil and filled with sin.

Noah was good, his heart was kind,
He had a pure and godly mind.

He told the people to listen to him,
And to refrain from all their evil and sin.

But they didn't like what he preached and said,
Many would have liked to have him dead.

He told them about God and the angels too,
But how many believed? Only a few.

But Noah continued to speak and teach,
Soon God ordered him not to preach.

He ordered him to build a ship,
That would hold animals inside it.

By God, Noah was informed,
That there would be a raging storm.

And so Noah built the ark,
And all the animals did embark.

They came together, two by two,
All the species, old and new,

And finally, when the boat was filled,
A storm came that made it tilt.

Torrents of rain came down from the sky,
But the ark went sturdily sailing by.

Noah just stared as the people drowned,
He heard their screams all around.

"Noah, Noah, save us," they cried,
But he shook his head and quietly sighed.

He saw his son on a rock very soon,
Clutching it hard, awaiting his doom.

Noah cried, "I wish I could save my son from sin,"
But a wave swept by, and his son fell in.

Then he heard his pleading cry,
Noah looked on, and bid him goodbye.

When all the evil-doers were dead,
God looked at Noah, and then He said:

"Noah! I will take you to dry land,"
Then He lifted the ark with his Mighty hand.

Noah's work was finally done,
He had destroyed the sinners – everyone.

ISLAM

In the lonely desert of the midday sky,
A silent town on the sands does lie.

A speck of life in a desert of death,
A desert that speaks despair with its every breath.

And in this silent, quiet town,
Not a soul is seen all around.

Except for a man, isolated, alone,
Weariness seeps from his every bone.

A river of blood flows from his head,
A hot, sticky river of red.

His eyes are closed with this killing pain,
His pious heart speaks in Allah's name.

His beaten up body is weary and weak,
Out of exhaustion his lips can't speak.

For help this godly man can't call,
He cannot move from where he did fall.

Some people come, they see him there.
They laugh and jeer, they do not care.

He feels a stone hit hard on his back,
It lands on the earth with a slap.

Then he hears tiny footsteps running across the sands,
He feels hot tears and a tiny hand,

Which wipes his tears and blood away.
He hears an innocent heart silently pray.

He rises slowly and holds her hand;
Together they walk across the golden sand.

His mission still remains undone,
To spread Islam this Prophet has come.

The people of Mecca try to tear his life apart,
But God infuses strength in his lonely heart.

Every day he tries again and again,
The people ridicule the Islamic name.

But slowly the number of Muslims grow,
Tortures and pain they come to know.

A Muslim slave is lashed again and again,
He is made to work to the point of pain.

"Who is your god?" his master cries,
"Allah," the godly Muslim slave replies.

The whip comes down hard upon his back,
This pious Muslim slave is black.

He is made to lie under the scorching heat,
Upon the boiling sand on which the sun does beat.

With bricks piled high upon his chest,
This Muslim slave knows no rest.

Muslims are tortured everywhere,
Their beaten bodies lie here and there.

But these godly Muslims, they do not fight,
Even though they have the right.

They listen and wait for God's word,
He has ordered them not to take up the sword.

They bear patiently the insults and pain,
They feel they will never know peace again.

So my friends, listen well,
You've heard of what I've had to tell.

Islam was spread by peaceful means,
Not by violence as it so seems.

To end cruelty and torture Islam came,
Upholding peace and justice is Islam's aim.

O people try to undersand Islam,
It is indeed *not* a religion of harm.

Islam for faith and justice does stand,
It is a religion you must understand.

The Muslims spread Islam by suffering pain,
Suffering insults for Islam's name.

But slowly Islam spreads further still,
Yet many Muslims are even killed.

The Prophet and the Muslims leave this Meccan town,
Where there are cruelties all around.

They go to spread the message of justice in another place,
Where people welcome its Holy face.

Into the dark night the Prophet leaves,
While the town of Mecca does silently sleep.

O my Prophet, Islam will spread,
Do not worry your lonely head.

Go now to Medina and spread Islam,
One day nations will understand the one and only ISLAM.

THE LAST PROPHET

In the desert land of Arabia a child was born,
Whose father had died before he was born.

The land was evil and filled with sin,
Not even a place of goodness within.

The weak were killed by the wicked and strong,
There was no law against evil and wrong.

Baby girls were buried alive,
Some were saved and did survive;

But they were despised all around.
Wherever you looked there were sins to be found.

Now this child grew up amongst all this sin,
Yet he did not inhale any in.

He spoke the truth and did no wrong,
His heart was pure and his will was strong.

The things that were done were bad he knew,
Killing and looting he hated too.

Amena was his mother mild.
He was her only child.

His grandfather was so good and wise,
He turned away from sins and lies.

His uncle was the chief of the clan,
He was a good and pious man.

The truthful and trustworthy, the child was known,
He became good at trade as he had grown.

The child grew older now a man.
And then one day according to Allah's plan,

He met a lady Khadija by name.
Her heart was pure and free from blame,

She was gentle, her temper mild,
As pure and good as a new born child.

She loved good and hated sin,
She loved all those who had goodness in.

She asked this man to help her trade,
And so an honest profit he made.

Janab-e-Khadija wasted no time,
She'd studied enough this figure sublime.

They were married and were happy too,
And from them a great generation grew.

One night this man returned home with fever
From the famous cave of Hira.

To pray to God he'd gone up there,
Far far away from every where.

As he entered the house he let out a cry.
Khadija rushed to him and asked him why.

Quivering and quaking he replied:
"I prayed in Hira for a day and a night,

When a beautiful man appeared before me,
He was an angel, that I could see,

'Iqra bisme rabbukal lazi' [1]
Is then what he said to me.

I repeated the words and rushed home.
I feel so worried and very alone."

FOOTNOTE

1. Holy Quran Chapter 96 Verse 1 meaning "Read thou in the name of the Lord who created."

Khadija assured him, he had committed no sin,
So this must be something good for him.

He was now a Prophet she soon knew,
She was pleased and happy too.

The Prophet had to preach Islam,
And to pull away people from worldly harm.

Three years later at least,
The Prophet invited many men to feast.

The Prophet invited them for a day,
So they might follow him in his way.

When the prophet asked if they would,
Only Ali wholeheartedly stood.

The rest laughed at him and mocked him too,
But his preaching only grew and grew.

More people believed in what he said,
They were the ones who used their head.

The Meccans begged him not to preach Islam,
Mecca would certainly come to harm,

They offered him anything if only he stopped,
Mecca would certainly come to rot.

He was firm, his will was strong,
He refrained from doing any wrong.

"If you put the sun in my right hand, the moon in my left,
Still from my stand I would never drift,"

So the people tortured him and his followers too,
The tortures grew and grew and grew.

So the Prophet sent some followers far away,
To Abyssinia is what the Muslims say,

To spread his religion everywhere,
Islam is for the world to share.

Now more in Medina had accepted Islam,
And was inviting the Prophet to spread its charm.

They invited him to Medina to settle too,
They invited his Meccan followers too.

So he sent his Meccan followers on,
From Mecca to Medina they had gone.

And then one night the Prophet rode,
Far away from his Meccan abode.

Leaving the brave Ali in his bed,
'Now' the Meccans couldn't follow his tread.

Meccan *Muhajir*[1] and Medinite *Ansar*,[2]
One *Muhajir* brother of one *Ansar*.

Together against invaders the Muslims fought,
And victory to Islam and God they brought.

Badr, Khandaq, Khayber and Honain,
Were the victories the Muslims gained.

Sad at suffering so much defeat,
The Meccans signed a treaty of peace.

The treaty was broken hardly two years later,
By the cruel Meccan idolators.

The bloodless conquest of Mecca was then declared,
And of all the false gods the *Kaaba*[3] was cleared.

Truth has come and falsehood gone,
Islam has come to clear all wrong.

The Prophet wished to preach Islam,
So he invited some Christians from Najran.

FOOTNOTES

1. Muslim migrants to Medina.
2. Helphers – the Medinite Muslim residents.
3. Muslim sacred building at Mecca, 'the holy of holies'.

The Christians and Muslims sat down to speak,
Soon the talk became rather bleak.

They came to a point where they didn't agree,
So a *Mubahala* [1] there was to be.

From the Prophet's side five people went,
Five people whom God had sent,

Whom God had filled with perfect purity,
The Prophet, Hasnain,[2] Fatima and Ali.

Nearness to God was what the Christians saw,
In the face of the Prophet and the other four;

And so from *Mubahala* they declined,
As the wrath of God came to their mind.

On the Prophet's last pilgrimage to Mecca and back,
The Prophet proclaimed on a camel's back.

"O' Muslims you will never go astray,
If you listen to what I have to say.

You must obey my *Ahl-e-bait* [3] and Holy Quran,
And all the Heavenly laws of Islam.

These two will never separate from each other,
And will meet me at the paradise river.

Remember the rights of women and slaves,
You will answer your wrongs inside your graves,

But the most important thing for Muslims and Islam,
Is to accept Ali as *Maula* [4] of those whose *Maula* I am.

'I have perfected your religion this very day'." [5]
This was the last message of God that day.

FOOTNOTES

1. With mutal agreement to invoke curse of God on the liar. See Holy Quran Chapter 3 Verses 58-60.
2. Hasan and Husain, the grandsons of the Prophet.
3. The daughter, the son-in-law and the grandsons of the Prophet.
4. Guardian, leader.
5. Holy Quran Ch 5 Verse 3.

The Prophet's journey to paradise was very near,
He returned to God the following year.

THE REVELATION

Hate gleams like fire in his cruel eyes
Oblivious to his daughter's unceasing cries.
With brutal force he digs at the sand,
Anger disclosed in his destructive hand.
Quickly, he puts the babe in the ground.
The girl utters not a sound,
Then she laughs – Is this a game?
But her father sneers "I'll not have people insult
my name."
"Die girl die – I'll not let you live.
Let this grave be forever your crib."
The babe laughs innocently – still unaware.
He covers the babe without a care.
Then suddenly she begins to cry,
Her father taunts "Die girl die"
Then as he finishes burying the babe,
He turns quickly and walks away.

Time passes – silence settles in the air,
The mound of earth remains untouched and bare.

Soon it is seen by a passer-by,
Who suddenly lets out a startled cry
He knows that someone's baby girl is there
Buried alive by a custom unfair.
Rushing to the place, he starts to dig,
"Please O please, let her live."

But the baby child – she is dead,
The man cries and holds his head,
Why O why are these people so cruel?
Why must they let aggression rule?
The man's face with nobility shines,
His eyes as well glisten and shine –
With tears of regret at what these people do,
Whose evils are many and good deeds few.
Surely there must be a way to make this evil stop.
Slowly the man makes his way to the mountain top.
And in a silent cave, he sits in peace,
And thinks as to how he can make these evils cease.

Suddenly the cave is filled with a luminous light,
And a being appears before his sight

"Read" the magnificent being commands,
"I cannot read" the frightened man returns.
Then with a force, the being says:
"Read in the name of thy Lord,
Who created –
Created man out of a clot:
And taught man that which he knew not."[1]

With trembling voice, and fear in his eyes,
The man repeats what the being says.
Then when the being disappears,
The man shakes with apprehension and fear.
Quivering and trembling, he quickly climbs down,
He is filled with a fear he has never known.
He stumbles and falls in the busy streets,
With terror and anguish his heart beats.
And with sudden speed he enters his home,
During this time, his anxiety has grown.
Worried, his wife rushes to his side,
"Dear husband why do you look so tired,
Why do your eyes with horror, stare and see,
And your body shake like a leaf on a tree?
Dear husband, please please do tell
And rest a while – you look not well."
With tremor in his voice, and worry in his eyes
The pious trembling man replies:
"Good wife, today I saw something I never saw
  before,
A thing that filled me with fear and awe.
I saw before me a being appear,
A being so magnificent, he filled me with fear.
He illuminated the cave's dark and sinister gloom,
And stared at me with eyes like the fiery noon.
I could not meet that fiery gaze,
And fell to the floor in an awe-stricken daze.
'Read' he suddenly commandingly cried,
'I cannot read' I with fear replied.
Then that being said to me:
'Iqra bisme rabbokal lazi'[2]
I repeated the words and rushed home,
I feel so worried and very alone."

FOOTNOTES

1. Holy Quran Ch. 96 Verses 1-5.
2. Holy Quran Ch. 96 Verse 1.

"My dear husband" his wife replies,
"Don't worry yourself or tremble and sigh,
You have never committed a sin,
Your heart is pure and good within,
Your tongue is truthful, your mind wise and pure.
Something good has happened, of that I am sure."

Slowly a smile appears on the godly face,
Of worry there remains but a little trace.
And slowly he falls into the realms of sleep,
Into the gentle loving arms of peace.
While his good wife thinks, "I must find out,
We must know what this is all about."
So quiet and silent as a mouse,
Thc lady leaves her humble house.
And goes to her uncle, old and frail,
And asks him the meaning of this strange tale.
With a happy sparkle in his eyes,
The old man joyfully cries:
"Rejoice dear niece, your husband is the one,
Whose goodness and piety is second to none,
Whose every action is loved by the Lord,
Who acts in goodness and is true to his word,
Surely your husband is the chosen man,
A Prophet of God and a gift to man."
The lady is filled with a sudden delight,
Happiness and joy stands before her sight,
With joy in her step and light in her eye,
She thankfully bids her uncle goodbye.
She rushes home to tell the good news,
And awakens her husband from his snooze:
"My good husband, awake and arise,
I bring good news to lighten your eyes:
A Prophet of God, my husband you are,
For your peity excels all others by far."
Soon by God our Prophet is told,
To let the religion of God unfold,
And to let the riches of Islam spread,
To every heart and to every head.

HIJRAT AND THE CONQUEST OF MECCA

The night is dark, there is a chill of air,
A deadly silence hangs everywhere.

A sword glimmers in the night so deep,
While a brave youth lies asleep.

Forty swordsmen lie 'round the house,
Every man as quiet as a mouse.

But the youth – he sleeps and doesn't wake,
He defends the Prophet whose life's at stake.

The Prophet – he leaves the house alone,
He leaves the house that is his home.

He is the one the men want to kill,
But he leaves the house because God has willed.

The men – they do not see him leave,
His shoulder touches, they do not feel.

They do not see on God's accord,
Anything's possible by will of the Lord.

He travels on, in the cover of night,
And rests when the sun gives out its light.

He's left Mecca, where he's lived so long,
He'd tried to prevent the people from wrong.

Many Meccans didn't like what he said,
They wanted him and his followers dead.

They tortured the Muslims, with methods cruel;
They starved the slaves of food and fuel.

They spread thorns in his path, and thorns by his
door,
But his love for God grew ever more.

His followers stood firm, with hearts so strong,
They continued to refrain, from sin and wrong.

So now they'd left Mecca to be far away,
To Medina they'd gone, to preach and stay.

Soon he nears the Medinite's town,
Outside the City there is a throng.

The poeple rejoice, as they see him come,
The man they've wished to see so long.

They wave, and laugh, and rejoice and cheer,
"Muhammad is here! Muhammad is here!"

He's hungry and thirsty, the heat is strong,
He comes from the desert to preach against wrong.

The Muslims increase, as the years go by.
But the Muslims remember with a sigh,

The Meccan town they'd left behind;
Which still lives firmly, in their mind.

They long to see those Meccan streets,
To call back those memories.

And they so long to see once more,
The House of God, as before.

Muhammad senses, they wish to go,
And proclaims to them it will be so.

He makes sure that they know,
Their weapons would be very few.

To show the Meccans they want no war,
They come only to see Mecca once more.

And so they go, on their way,
With a spirit of faith that does not sway.

When they reach, those Meccan gates,
The inhabitants of Mecca make them wait.

So in Hudaibia, they camp for the night,
Signing a treaty by lantern light.

His message now spreads, like a flowing tide,
To many countries far and wide.

That treaty of peace, the Meccans break,
Thus the voice of God does speak.

The Muslims enter Mecca with heads held high,
Pride in their hearts, and tears in their eye.

The Meccans hide, as they see them come,
Thousands of Muslims – their hearts joined as one.

Into Mecca, those Muslims ride,
Their eyes twinkle, with tears of pride.

They remember the days, that they had spent,
With their families, and their friends.

They remember the days, when they accepted Islam.
When they were tortured, when they were harmed.

When out of their families, they were cast away,
When out of their homes, they were chased away.

When they were stoned outside the town,
When companions fell painfully to the ground.

O' they remember those days so well,
Each heart has a painful story to tell.

How he was treated in this beloved town,
How his fellow Muslims were burnt to the ground.

Yet now they come, marching in,
Their souls fighting the evil and sin.

They wish to kill not man, woman or child,
Those brave Muslims are strong yet mild.

But a clash of swords, there has been,
By Khalid's regiment there is death to be seen.

The tragic news to the Prophet arrives,
The Prophet frowns and lets out a sigh.

The loss of life is very small,
But the Prophet aims to console them all.

He sends Ali, to compensate,
To calm their fury, and their hate.

The Muslims then go to the House of the Lord,
In which the idols have been stored.

The Holy Prophet steps in with pride,
And breaks down the idols that are inside.

Tumbling and crashing the idols come to the floor,
Yet there are left still some more.

They are piled way up high,
He makes up his mind with determination in his eye.

To climb on his shoulders, he asks Ali,
And break down the idols that sit with glee.

So the House of God is pure again,
Cleansed by two noble men.

IMAM ALI

A very brave man was Ali,[1]
The Lion of God, the Prophet's *Wasi*.[2]

His father was the chief of the clan,
He was a good and pious man.

His mother was entirely free from blame.
Fatima, *bint-e* Asad was her name.

His cousin, the Prophet, was brought up by these two.
Children they'd had and quite a few too.

In *Kaaba* our first *Imam* was born,
Near the very early hours of dawn.

When his eyes opened for the very first time,
He was met with the Prophet's face sublime.

The Prophet wished to adopt Ali,
To relieve his guardians of a responsibility.

Once the Prophet had a feast,
With a tiny amount of things to eat.

Some meat, some bread and some milk to drink,
Filled the appetites to the brim.

But the food remained the same as before,
Not any less, not any more.

The invited men were from his kin,
He wanted them to repent their sin;

Advising them to accept the Faith,
And helping him to propagate.

FOOTNOTES

1. Cousin and son-in-law of the Holy Prophet Muhammad.
2. Executor.

When the Prophet asked if they would,
Only Ali whole-heartedly stood.

Gradually more people chose Islam,
So they might be free from every harm.

It was of course for their very own good,
Not only in this world but afterwards.

The Quraish[1] had troubled the Muslims
for a long time now;
How they survived! Only God knows how.

The Prophet's life was now at stake;
Ali thought and acted straight.

He did something very brave,
Which could have led him to the grave;

For on the Prophet's bed Ali slept,
While into the night the Prophet crept.

From Mecca to Medina the Prophet had gone.
He travelled by night and rested by dawn.

Soon Ali came to Medina too,
To unite with his cousin, the last *Rasool*.[2]

The Prophet made progress to preach Islam,
He also invited Christians from Najran.

The Christians and Muslims talked on and on,
The Christians insisted God had a son.

On this point the two sides didn't agree;
So a *Mubahala*[3] there was to be.

From the Prophet's side, five people went,
Five people whom God had sent,

FOOTNOTE

1. The most influential tribe of Arabia.
2. Messenger of God.
3. With mutual agreement to invoke curse of God on the liar.
See Holy Quran Chapter 3 Verses 58-60

One heavenly lady and four pious men,
The Prophet, Ali, Fatima and Hasnain.[1]

The five faces shone so radiantly,
That the Christians noticed this obviously.

And so from *Mubahala* they declined,
As the wrath of God came to their mind.

Ali was also one of the five under the *Kisa*,[2]
With the Prophet, Hasnain and Fatima.

"Whoever loves them loves me,
Blessings and purification I pray from Thee."

This is what the Prophet prayed for under the *Kisa*,
For Ali, Hasnain and Fatima.

The Prophet loved his *Ahl-e-bait*.
And about them he often said:

"My *Ahl-e-bait* are the Ark of Nooh,
The boat that will help to save you.

The strong rope of God that leads to the Heavens,
From the fire of Hell that menacingly threatens.

The door of forgiveness, the purified ones,
They will save fathers, mothers, daughters and sons."

Ali fought many battles again and again,
Badr, Ohad, Khandaq, Khayber and Honain.

Prophet loved Ali there is no doubt,
On many occasions he pointed out,

"I am the City of Knowledge and Ali is its Gate.
He is the most equitable judge, the embodiment of faith."

FOOTNOTES

1. Hasan and Husain, the grandsons of the Prophet.
2. It refers to an event when the Prophet collected his grandsons, his son-in-law and his daughter under a sheet with him and prayed to God to purify them with perfect purification and Verse 33 Ch. 33 of the Holy Quran was revealed.

On the Prophet's last pilgrimage to Mecca and back,
The Prophet proclaimed on a camel's back,

"I must tell you something before I depart,
My *Ahl-e-bait* and Quran will never part.

But the most important thing for Muslims and Islam,
Is to accept Ali as *Maula* of those whose *Maula* I am."

On the morn of 19th Ramadan,
When the *Moazzan*[1] gave the call for *Azan*,[2]

Ali knew that death was near,
Yet he went to the Mosque without any fear.

Suddenly a sword struck his head,
"By God I've reached my aim," he said.

Bin-e-Muljim did this dirty deed.
He tried to escape and ran to his steed.

He was caught and brought back to Ali,
Who ordered his ropes loose immediately.

Distrust came over Bin-e-Muljim,
When Ali offered some juice to him.

Ali looked sadly at the man,
Then he said, "O Abdul Rehman,[3]

If you had taken this drink from me,
Up in Heaven you'd be with me."

In two more days Ali was dead.
This was the day man really dread,

For centuries now man has wept.
While up in Heaven Ali has slept.

May Zainab[4] be blessed by Ali,
For this humble effort of poetry.

FOOTNOTES

1. The one who calls for prayer.
2. Call for prayer.
3. Bin-e-Muljim's name.
4. The poetess herself.

ALI'S MARTYDOM

Sleep reigned over the Kufan town,
As from the mosque came a godly sound.

The call for prayer filled the sky,
Moving the air with a gentle sigh.

Awakening Muslims with a gentle prod,
"O people come, and pray to God."

And in the silent mosque, Ali stood alone,
Gazing at every wall and stone.

He knew that these walls would be stained with blood,
Innocent, pious, saintly blood.

Today his blood would be shed,
These clean walls would be covered in red.

He was eager for martyrdom I am sure,
It was then he heard a tiny snore.

In a corner a sleeper lay,
Ali knew he had not come to pray.

Gently Ali awoke the man,
"Awake awake, O Abdul Rehman.

Come it is nearly time to pray,
Awake for the coming day.

I know your work, I know why you've come,
Remember your deed can not be undone."

Abdul Rehman nothing did say,
Quickly he rose and walked away.

Ali prepared for prayer as the Muslims came,
Ready to pray in Allah's name.

"Allah ho Akbar" his voice began,
Behind him stood Abdul Rehman.

"Allah ho Akbar" Ali said again,
And knelt before God with the other men.

Suddenly Abdul Rehman moved forward to kill,
His sword with poison was definitely filled.

He raised his sword and struck it down,
Confusion was there all around.

Ali's neck was covered with blood,
His head prostrated before his God.

Abdul Rehman quickly ran,
He was a scared and sinful man.

And Ali reeled back not crying out his pain,
His blood drenched lips spoke in Allah's name.

His heart felt happy, his mind so light,
He was finally ending his worldly life.

His sons held him in their arms,
As if to protect him from this physical harm.

His smiling lips parted and then he said,
"I thank Thee O Lord for a martyr's death."

Soon Abdul Rehman was brought before Ali,
His state was terrible Ali could see.

His bonds were cutting deep in his skin,
Causing the blood to spurt from within.

A frown creased Ali's brow,
He ordered the bonds be loosened NOW.

The murderer into tears broke,
Ali smiled faintly and then he spoke.

"It is not too late to repent O Abdul Rehman,
Was I an unjust or cruel Imam?"

Then to his sons Ali said,
"Give him a drink to relieve his head."

But Abdul Rehman did not trust Ali,
He refused the drink quietly.

Ali then spoke "O Abdul Rehman,
Why do you not trust your dying Imam?

If you had taken this juice of mine,
You'd be with me in Heaven divine."

In two more days Ali died,
With his mourning family by his side.

And the gates of Heaven opened and welcomed
him in,
Free was he from any stain of sin.

In the temporal sense, Ali is gone,
But his shining spirit and soul live on.

* * * * *

But one day Ali will leave Heaven's domain,
For sadness and misery and grief and pain.

His horse's hooves will gallop away from Heaven's
open door,
And touch the baking gold-dust floor.

To the land where there is nought but despair,
Where mutilated bodies will lie everywhere.

And by a river a blood drenched body will lie dead,
Sleeping the silent and sweet sleep of death.

And where this body will lie asleep,
Ali's sad eyes will silently weep.

Then he will gallop towards the burnt out camps,
And see a figure with sword in hand.

Her hair will be silver and her face sad and old,
As if within her she has griefs untold.

Approaching him, this lady will say,
"Turn your steed and go away!"

But inside Ali, grief will burn,
From this lady, he will not turn.

The lady his veiled face will not see,
"Go O stranger! Listen to me!"

But when Ali will take his veil away,
The lady will cry, and suddenly say,

"O my father! How late you have come!
See the evil that has been done!"

And she will tell of her griefs and pain,
And how she suffered in this wild terrain.

And when Ali will leave this sultry plain,
He will still be with Zainab in her trial of pain.

For with tied hands and broken heart,
She will bravely address those who had her hurt,

And her words will hang the people's heads in
shame,
Whilst her unshed tears will touch their hearts,

Like spears — leaving the scars of grief and shame
To dwell forever in their inner selves.

But in her every word they will remember Ali
Whose every word echoed the truth.

And the man whom they had thought was dead and
gone,
Will be alive and living in her once more . . .

So "Think not of those slain in the way of Allah as
dead.
Nay they are living, with the Lord they have
provision." [1]

FOOTNOTE

1. The Holy Quran Ch. 3 Verse 169.

JANAB-e-FATIMA

When Fatima was born, stars lit the sky,
Everything rejoiced, in the heavens, so high.

The angels were happy, and rejoiced as well,
And now about Fatima, I will tell:-

She was born in Mecca, this Lady Divine,
This wealthy lady, was ever so fine.

Her money was little, though her heart was filled
With kindness and love, and lots of goodwill.

Her father was a truthful man,
He was the last Prophet of Islam.

Her mother was so good and kind,
She was the perfect example of mankind.

When baby Fatima was only two,
Enmity against her father really grew.

He was beaten and whacked, and pushed around,
His half dead body laid on the ground.

She'd find and comfort, and bring him home,
To make him feel, he was not alone.

When he would put his head in his hands,
And sit helpless upon the burning sands.

Thinking his work was all a waste,
Tears rolling down his face.

A tiny hand would wipe them away,
And an innocent heart would silently pray.

But the Prophet's mission grew harder still,
Some of his followers were even killed.

So Fatima only at the age of two,
Along with the Prophet's followers too,

Went to a cave in the mountainside.
So they could be safe and quietly hide.

They stayed in the cave for three whole years,
At the end of their stay, Fatima shed tears.

For, her generous mother had finally died,
With her daughter, Fatima, by her side.

Three years later, when Fatima was eight,
The Prophet's life lay at stake.

The Meccans wished to stab him in bed,
They didn't want him preaching, but wanted him dead.

So when the people of Yasreb,[1] invited him to stay,
He left Mecca, and was on his way.

First he sent his followers on,
Then to Yasreb, he went on.

Fatima followed very soon,
She travelled under the light of the silvery moon.

Soon she arrived in Yasreb town,
And very quickly she settled down.

She married Ali, the first Imam,
And the first man to acknowledge Islam.

She bore two boys, Hasan and Husain,
They grew up to be two fine young men.

They went through lots of misery and gloom,
But they saved Islam from eternal doom.

Fatima grew wiser, as the years went on,
In the books of history, she has shone.

The figure of light was Fatima,
When she lay under the Holy *Kisa*.

FOOTNOTE

1. Another name of Medina.

When God purified her family,
The Prophet, Hasnain and Ali.

She was a lady, very pure,
Of that I'm certain, of that I'm sure.

On the *Mubahala*, she went too,
With Ali, Hasnain and the Last *Rasool.*

With Hasan clutching the Prophet's palm,
Husain cradled in the Prophet's arm.

Fatima walking behind the three,
And at the end walking Ali.

The five looked, so pure and clean,
Such Holy faces, were never seen.

The Christians knew, only truth they'd say,
So from *Mubahala* they backed away.

Then there came signs of a good Omen,
Soon Fatima, gave birth again.

First to Zainab, and then Kulsum,
Thus the Prophet's house did bloom.

With lots and lots, of happiness and love,
All sent down, from above.

But disaster struck – the Prophet grew ill,
He grew weak, and weaker still.

The Angel of Death was very near,
And over the Prophet, he did leer.

So with his daughter by his side,
The Holy Prophet finally died.

Fatima grew sad and very weak,
Her life grew dull, and really bleak.

Her fellow Muslims grew greedy and mean,
They stole the things that hers had been.

They didn't leave her husband alone,
They charged at him and charged his home.

And so by the Muslims, her life was torn,
They didn't leave her in peace to mourn.

One day Ali and Fatima were on their own,
Fatima standing by the door of her home.

When someone forced and broke down the door,
It struck the very child she bore.

Amazed Fatima, let out a cry,
She did faint, but the child did die.

Fatima grew weaker, as the days wore on,
She knew that soon, she would be gone.

And so she died, as she knew she would,
And her husband Ali, just sadly stood.

He buried her at the stroke of night,
When there was not a sign of light.

Thus the Leader of Women did die,
And in Jannatul Baqi, she does lie.

IMAM HASAN

Once Ummul Fazl[1] had a dream,
It was for her a horrible scene.

She dreamt a piece of the Prophet came to her home,
A small piece of his body, not his whole.

She was worried, and scared as well,
She didn't know what this dream did tell.

She asked the Prophet to help explain,
What was meant by the dream so strange.

He assured her happily, nothing was wrong,
And that his grandson, would be born.

He told her joyfully, that she would care
For the child so sweet and fair.

She was happy and very content,
And soon the babe from God was sent.

The first child of Ali and Fatima,
The babe was sent from Allah.

Soon an angel descended from high,
Shedding beautiful paths of light.

He joyfully told the people who came,
That Shabber or Hasan would be his name.

Hasan grew older and very wise,
His knowledge had an amazing size.

He would go to the Mosque and listen well,
To the things, the Prophet did tell.

He would listen and understand,
And thus his knowledge would expand.

FOOTNOTE

1. A close relative of the Prophet.

He went to *Mubahala* by the Prophet's side,
An honest face, with nothing to hide.

He lay under the Holy *Kisa*,
With the Prophet, Husain, Ali and Fatima.

When he was seven, his grandfather died,
Hasan was sad and often cried.

Three months later, his mother died too,
Now his sadness really grew.

But his father's troubles were even more,
Much much more than before.

When Hasan was older, his father died as well,
Hasan's misery, no one can tell.

God had proclaimed him to be Imam,
But Muawiyah was a terrible enemy of Islam.

Muawiyah wanted leadership, no matter what,
And innocent people, were murdered a lot.

Women and children were cruelly killed,
He bribed the people to do as he willed.

Muawiyah misled people, more and more,
Imam Hasan knew, there'd be war.

He knew that thousands would be killed,
If he did not have peace instilled.

So he persuaded Muawiyah, not to fight,
And a treaty of peace they did write.

They signed a treaty of peace for the land,
But Muawiyah ruled, with his evil band.

Imam Hasan, the second Imam,
Now began to preach Islam.

People began to understand,
What kind of person ruled the land.

Piety and kindness they came to know,
And the number of believers began to grow.

Muawiyah was angry and wanted this stopped,
Quietly he began to scheme and plot.

So Muawiyah conspired, with a wife of Hasan,
He wanted to end, the true Islam.

They talked and plotted with total glee,
An ungrateful wife of Hasan was she.

She took some poison, to poison him,
And then set out to do this sin.

The woman was bribed into doing this,
She was happy and full of bliss.

The money, she saw in her mind's eye,
She would receive it when the Imam died.

She took some water, and poured the poison in,
Her hand trembled, when doing this sin.

But to her the money was more sublime,
So she committed this hideous crime.

She gave him the water, with guilt in her head,
He drank it slowly, and soon he was dead.

He had been a man very brave,
Now he wished to be buried, by the Prophet's grave.

But soldiers kept his coffin away,
On that very sad, and tragic day.

So his body was taken to Jannatul Baqi,
Away from his grandfather the last *Nabi.*[1]

His brothers and sisters, sobbed and cried,
As he was laid, by his mother's side.

FOOTNOTE

1. Messenger of God.

So by his mother he now lies,
The Leader of the Youths of Paradise.[1]

FOOTNOTE

1. It is a saying of Prophet Muhammad (peace be upon him).

BACKGROUND INFORMATION

To fully understand my poems on the martyrs and events of Kerbala, I feel that it is necessary to give a brief historical background of the events leading to this confrontation.

Islam's message was delivered in a dark period of Arabian pagan history. It taught mankind the belief in one God and the compulsive practice of equality and justice between people of every colour and race. Naturally, Islam was seen as a threat by the privileged tribes and their leaders, and was violently and stubbornly opposed by them. Like all the other messengers of God, the last messenger of God suffered immensely at their hands – Muslims were tortured, excommunicated and eventually forced to migrate to Medina. Even in Medina, Islam's adversaries persistently waged wars against them. However, these pagans repeatedly suffered defeat at the hands of the followers of Islam. It was only after Mecca had fallen to the Muslims, that Abu-Sufyan, the arch enemy of Islam, realised that he would be unable to maintain any powerful position over the people as a non-Muslim, and so he embraced Islam, only two years before the Prophet's death. The enmity from without was not as dangerous as the enmity from within. Nearly two years after the Prophet's death, Abu-Sufyan succeeded in obtaining material gains for himself and the status of governors of Jordan and Syria for his two sons. After the death of his brother, Muawiyah became the governor of both Jordan and Syria. Within only thirty years after the death of the prophet, Muawiyah managed to become the ruler of the Muslim Empire. During the governorship of Abu-Sufyan's sons and Muawiyah's rule, the same old pagan values and practices became prevalent with one difference that now they were made to appear as Islamic values because the ruler had declared himself a Muslim. The Holy Prophet Muhammad's hard labour was being undone.

Muawiyah now designated his son, Yazid – a debauchee – as his heir, and forced the Muslims to offer their allegiance to him. Six people refused. The grandson of the Prophet, Imam[1] Husain, was the most important amongst them. Muawiyah realised that the Imam was highly respected as a pious and righteous Muslim, and forcing him to offer allegiance could create an explosive situation. Hence, he preferred to use his usual method of secret murder to eliminate his opposition. However, he died before being able to carry out his plan. His son, Yazid, not as clever, but equally ambitious, succeeded him. He insisted that Imam Husain should offer him his allegiance; because allegiance from him would mean certifying his corrupt rule as Islamic. Naturally, the Imam refused, and by doing so, clearly showed the *Ummah* (Muslim nation) that the actions of every Muslim are not necessarily Islamic.

At the request for guidance from the Iraqi people, the Imam, to avoid secret murder, proceeded towards Iraq with a few relatives, friends, ladies and children. The Imam took the ladies and children firstly because he wanted to show that his intentions were peaceful and secondly because he had realised the extent of the Caliph's barbaric nature and knew that he would be confronted and eventually martyred. He realised that after him, it would be these very ladies and children who, through their words and sufferings would disclose to the people the paganism of the 'Muslim' Caliph. As he had predicted, the Imam was eventually confronted by the multitudes of Yazid's army and was informed that if he offered allegiance to Yazid, he would be left unharmed. However, the Imam refused, and was consequently martyred along with his friends and relatives. Only his ill son survived – he was made to trudge on foot through Kufa and Damascus while the ladies and children were mounted on the bare backs of camels and paraded through the bazaars.

The dead Imam's grief stricken sister, Janab-e-Zainab, in speeches in these bazaars and courts,

FOOTNOTE

1. The word Imam has two meanings – literal and specific. Literally Imam means leader. The specific meaning of Imam refers to divine leadership bestowed by God on twelve descendents of the Holy Prophet Muhammad by virtue of their piety, knowledge and infallibility.

informed the people that they were the grandchildren of the Prophet and that the cause of the Imam was to retain the values of Islam which were being distorted by the existing so called Muslim rulers of the nation. She informed them how, for this cause he had sacrificed his own life as well as the lives of those whom he loved. She also revealed the tortures they had suffered at the hands of Yazid's army which violated beyond expectation the teachings of the Holy Prophet. This left the *Ummah* in no doubt about the fact that the Muslim rulers were indeed attempting to revive the old pagan ideals under the name of Islam. The result was that the Caliph was put under immense pressure by the people and even by one of his own wives and her son. The captives were set free, the existing dynasty was shattered and the corrupt leaders were forced to leave their high offices.

It is remarkable that the rule of such a powerful ruler could not even withstand the words of a lady bound by the ropes of captivity. Yet what is there that is unremarkable about the tragedy of Kerbala? Indeed, it is a tragedy that baffles the writer and cripples the hand of the poet. A tragedy that reveals how the weak conquered the powerful; how those that died, lived eternally and how those that faced disgrace and humiliation rose in dignity and honour.

Zainab Kazim.

IMAM HUSAIN

Pains are suffered of course,
When fighting against the evil force.

Hunger and thirst in the scorching sun,
For three days one by one.

When you see your nephew, you remember your brother,
And now he appears with his martyrdom's letter.[1]

Seeing your brother's writing, you let out a sob,
You allow your nephew to go to God.

You hear his cry and know he's dead.
All over the place his body is spread.

It's been trampled over by the hooves of horses,
By the cruel wicked evil forces.

And down by the river side,
Lies a brave youth so gallant and mild.

His arms cut off, an arrow in his eye,
Slowly his life goes passing by.

And by his side is a waving banner,
In a brilliant and very noble manner.

And even if your eldest son has a spear in his chest,
You must still stick to what is best.

Your baby son is lying asleep.
He looks holy but frail and weak.

FOOTNOTE

1. Imam Hasan at his death bed had given a letter for his son to open it when in great difficulty. In Kerbala when Imam Husain was reluctant to give his nephew permission to fight, his nephew opened the letter of his father. That letter was addressed to his brother Husain stating that his son would be representing him in Kerbala and asked to permit him to fight.

You must get him water before he dies.
You pick him up from where he lies.

To bring enemies to your side will be your main aim,
With this holy baby free from blame.

You make your way to the enemy ranks;
They may give him water from the river banks.

They reply by shooting this ghastly arrow,
Which arrives in his neck so frail and narrow.

As you leave your tents the ladies cry;
You look at them sadly letting out a sigh.

For them you know what lies in store,
As the Holy Prophet had said before.

You have confidence but just the same,
You remind your sister to complete your aim.

You look at your daughter knowing she'll die;
You blink back a tear that comes to your eye.

You know she'll suffer worse than the others;
You know she'll miss all her brothers.

Your ladies' *chadars* [1] will be snatched away,
They'll be presented in bazaars on the way.

You don't falter, you don't turn,
At any cost you don't return.

But your ladies'll uphold justice and in faith they'll shine;
Even if they suffer humiliation by cruel rulers of the time.

I know this history very well;
But the rest for me is hard to tell.

You gallop ahead and know you'll die;
Your throat and mouth feel very dry;

FOOTNOTE

1. Scarves or covering sheets.

You stop fighting peaceful content;
You've completed your mission for which you were sent.

In your mind you hear *Azan*;
You prostrate before God and pray for Islam.

You feel a blade that really burns,
To God we belong and to Him we return.

THE SACRIFICE

Along the desert's lonely sands,
A scorching sun stretched baking hands.

As a lonely group trudged along,
With a spirit that kept their hearts so strong.

As they neared their destiny,
A cloud of dust they did see.

A rumble in the earth and a tremor in the air,
A tired, thirsty army began to near.

They were hot and thirsty and parched,
A sip of water was all they asked.

Their hands trembled, they could barely stand,
Upon that baking, scorching sand.

The small group's leader looked at them,
He welcomed them like long lost friends.

He offered them all the water he had,
But the General looked old, and weak and sad.

When the group's leader asked full of concern,
The General said the group must return.

The General said he couldn't let them go on,
He'd been ordered to kill if they went on.

The group's leader knew the General meant well,
He knew this very well.

He looked in the distance, far away,
What he saw he didn't say.

Not the boiling, scorching, baking sand,
Not Kufa, or Medina, but another land.

He saw death, he saw sorrow,
He knew he would see Kerbala tomorrow.

But he smiled to the General, his new found friend,
"Goodbye Hur we will meet again."

CONFLICT WITHIN

Darkness shrouds the sinister sky.
The wind reels back with a tormented sigh.

The desert lies barren like an empty grave.
Its gold dust the empty earth does pave.

The silver river lies silent and pure;
She is heartless indeed – a fiend demure!

Speak O Evil One, how canst thou flow?
Children die, dost thou not know?

In that lonely desert where thou dost weave,
How canst thou little children bereave?

"It is not I," she seems to say,
"Look yonder O person, and from me – away!"

And as I squint through the mist of sand,
I see sleeping tents and a lone man.

His worried face contorted with pain.
Trembling hands he cannot contain.

Like a caged lion pacing the ground.
His mouth uttering but an anguished sound;

"Why O why?" he does demand,
"Why did I give that fatal command?

Blindly I followed the Caliph's whim –
Oblivious was I of my fatal sin.

The Imam's kindness, I abhorred,
The path of truth, I ignored.

No mercy or piety did I show,
No compassion of heart did I bestow.

Of water I deprived his kith and kin –
My parched body was an ocean of sin.

Heedless was I to my heartless crime,
While my Imam, he remained pious, sublime.

Towards me he stretched a loving hand –
An oasis was he in a barren land.

To my harsh commands, he replied with a smile,
"Hur my friend, come rest a while."

Because of me, he is in a hostile land,
My dear Imam with his faithful band.

Surrounded by this tumultuous hoarde,
No food or water has he stored.

My Lord have mercy upon my soul!
Clear to me is my ultimate goal –

These hoardes of evil, I must defy,
For my Imam, I must die."

SAQQA-E-SAKINA
(The water carrier of Sakina)

Sparkling, silvery, flowing and free,
The silent river Furat was she;

A graceful river in a baking land,
A golden sun burning yellow sand.

An oasis in a parched and barren space,
Her gentle movements so out of place.

Her sparkling water like glitter glowed
As through the sand she softly flowed.

But away from her gently rippling tide,
Away from her silent riverside,

A bloody battle raged on.
Many young innocents were dead and gone.

And outside a tent on which the sun did beat,
Sakina laid a bag at her uncle's feet.

Her lips were parched, her throat was dry,
She looked at her uncle with hope in her eye.

His heart ached at the state she was in,
Her innocent mind immune from sin.

He promised her that he would quench her thirst,
After securing permission first.

And so Abbas entered the battlefield,
A spear in his hand and God as his shield.

Islam's noble banner close to his heart
And an empty waterbag dear to his heart.

Astride a noble, valiant beast,
He charged through the enemies;

A youth charging through the cowardly ranks,
Eager to reach the river banks.

Quickly he descended from his lofty mare
And filled the bag – so dry and bare,

Took some water in his cupped hand,
Then angrily threw it upon the sand.

How could he think of quenching his thirst,
When the children still for water did thirst?

He allowed his horse to have a drink,
But it turned it's face and looked at him.

"How can I drink?" it seemed to say,
"Our master still thirsts, let's be on our way."

So with waterbag filled he jumped astride,
With one thought only on his mind:

To get the water to the camp so near –
To the innocent ones he held so dear.

Seeing him gallop towards the camp,
Someone shouted from the enemy ranks.

Man after man came to fight,
It was indeed an amazing sight.

Abbas fought on so valiant and brave,
Like his father Ali who lay in his grave.

Courageously the youth fought on and on,
Protecting the waterbag all along.

The enemies knew they fought in vain,
They fired arrows again and again.

Abbas glanced up towards the sky,
He saw the sharpened arrows fly.

He bent across the waterbag,
Arrow after arrow ripped through his back.

The arrows pierced his legs, back and head,
The lone warrior was cloaked in red.

He saved the waterbag from coming to harm,
But suddenly a man cut off his arm.

Abbas clutched the banner in his teeth so tight.
He gave a brave and spirited fight.

He must get the water back,
He must protect the waterbag.

Someone slashed off his other arm;
The waterbag must not come to harm.

As he galloped on, he murmured a prayer,
Of his life he didn't care.

"To complete my mission, O Allah help me."
But this was certainly not to be.

Suddenly an arrow flew across the golden sky,
It pierced the bag, and the soldier did sigh.

The sparkling silver water gushed out,
The water was gone, there was no doubt.

Anguished, Abbas let out a cry,
Seeing the water his hopes did die.

Wounded he fell upon the burning sand,
Upon the barren and scorching sand.

"O my master here I lie,
Come to me before I die."

He heard footsteps, his master had come,
"Abbas! Abbas! What have they done?"

Husain's heart with anguish did cry,
Watching his brother's life go passing by.

His aged eyes shed streaming tears,
His shattered heart cried out its fears.

"O my master," Abbas gently said,
"There are some wishes I would like to express.

When I was born, it was your face I saw,
And now that I die on this river shore,

It is your face that I wish to see.
Master clear my eye so I can see

And do not carry my body when I die,
Let this be the place where I lie.

This is the place where I must rest,
I cannot face Sakina, even in death."

Into tears Husain broke,
But controlling his sobs, he quietly spoke.

"You've called me 'Master' since childhood to date,
Now call me 'Brother' with your dying breath."

With streaming tears, Husain cleared his brother's eye,
"My brother, My brother," Abbas said with a gentle sigh.

Then by the river he passed away,
Husain's unconscious body on top of him lay.

And the silver river murmured its protest,
A silent, angry tidal object,

For killing the lion of Kerbala,
Kerbala, O Kerbala, O Kerbala . . .

BABY MARTYR IN THE CAMP

In an angry mist of baking sand,
A tent stood upon the barren land.

Inside this tent a mother did pray,
As in a cradle a baby lay.

His face so sweet, and pious, and pure,
A mother could surely want nothing more.

But his young life was passing by,
Inside his mouth, his tongue lay dry.

His little body was frail and hot,
As he lay inside his tiny cot,

The mother looked at her six month child,
So innocent, so young, so small, so mild.

Hoping and wishing with all her heart,
That the enemy would some water impart.

Every minute that went again,
Was full of torture, anguish and pain.

She held her baby with tears in her eye,
She knew he was about to die.

In anguish lay her heart and mind,
As a noise came from behind.

Imam Husain entered the tent,
To his side she quickly went.

"O Master get water for my little babe,"
She with hope and anguish prayed.

Gently and quickly, Husain replied,
"I'll get him water from the other side."

"Give my little baby Asghar to me,
To the enemy, I will appeal.

They might spare his innocent life,
And give him water from the river side."

Slowly Husain took Asghar in his arms,
Away from his mother's appealing charms.

"Sire go quickly, time goes fast,
My little baby might not last."

So Hussain took little Asghar outside,
Shading the baby with his cloak out wide.

To protect him from the burning sun,
His young, innocent, beautiful son.

The enemy was guarding the river bank,
A murmur arose from their ranks.

What was this Husain held in his hands?
Some thought it was the Holy Quran.

But when he took the cloak away,
A hush fell in an awed way.

Husain held the baby aloft,
The baby's tongue was dry and soft.

He held the babe for all to see,
And with a loud and noble voice said he:

"O soldiers of Damascus you have betrayed me,
You've killed my friends and my family.

And now I hold my babe up high,
O soldiers how can you let him die?

With innocence this little bud does burst,
I ask you soldiers to quench his thirst."

Then he whispered in his baby's ear,
"O my son listen and hear.

Show them my son how you thirst,
Show them my son how much you thirst."

The baby turned his tiny face,
His pure body so out of place.

He passed his tongue across his lips,
Showing them he wanted some water to sip.

Then Husain put the babe upon the sand,
A murmur arose in the enemy rank.

Soldiers turned their faces away,
Hiding the tears that suddenly came.

The General sensed something was wrong,
What had happened to his army so strong?

Angrily he ordered Hurmula to shoot,
He was deadly dangerous and acute.

Without waiting a moment, Hurmula shot,
At the babe who lay on the sand so hot.

But Husain had removed the baby from the sand,
And the arrow fell on the yellow land.

Where only a tiny moment ago,
A child had lain, silently so.

Hurmula aimed, again once more,
Determined not to miss like before.

He saw a veiled figure this time,
It was the anxious mother sublime.

He hesitated with the arrow and bow,
His hesitancy began to grow.

Then he shot with an unsteady hand,
He missed, and the arrow fell upon the sand.

Then Hurmula hardened his wicked mind,
Cruel, nasty, evil, unkind.

The arrow travelled fast and true,
Into the baby's tender neck too.

The red blood gushed out,
From the enemy came a victory shout.

Husain's tears flowed free,
O Allah how could this be?

How low can these people stoop?
This large, ugly, wicked group.

Husain, the little baby cloaked,
It was with blood and tears soaked.

Should he bury the baby here?
Or should he show him to his mother so dear.

Hesitating, he walked on,
Then walked back from where he'd gone.

He hesitated again and again,
Then he walked towards the tent.

The mother glanced at the father's face,
She looked at his aged tear streaked face.

Husain uncovered the little baby so,
His uncontrollable grief did so grow.

His wife fainted then and there,
Life was so cruel and unfair.

Slowly Husain walked outside,
With heart filled misery he cried and cried.

Husain alone, sad and brave,
Dug a tiny little grave.

He put the little baby in,
The tiny bloodstained baby in.

Slowly he covered the miniature grave,
His lonely heart sad and brave.

Then he looked towards the sky,
Bidding his babe in Heaven goodbye.

THE MASOOM[1]

In the malicious, sweltering, unbearable heat
Stood a proud, noble, valiant beast.

Upright and dignified a horse did stand,
His hooves digging in the simmering sand.

Upon the barren land of Kerbala,
Stood this noble horse, Zuljana.

And on the sand by his feet,
A little child did so weep.

Her little arms clutching his legs so tight,
"O Zuljana, don't take my father to fight."

Her innocent heart was broken apart,
Her tiny, innocent, virtuous heart.

With little sobs, this child did cry,
Her tears were like pearls in her eye.

Her tears like rivers on her cheeks did flow,
With childhood's purity this young one did glow.

"O Zuljana, don't take my father to die,"
Sakina did so sob and cry.

Then she heard footsteps upon the sand
And felt strong, loving, fatherly hands.

Father held daughter close to his heart,
The two felt they could never part.

Sobbing painfully the two did cry,
"O my father don't go to die."

The father kissed the innocent head,
Then with a painful sigh he sadly said,

"My dearest child, how can I explain?
I must go to fight in Allah's name.

FOOTNOTE

1. Innocent, sinless.

Child you are yet too young to understand,
But against this evil, I must take a stand.

So my dear child, let me die,
And with a smile bid me goodbye."

They held each other in an embrace,
Then Sakina stared at her father's face.

Then very softly Sakina spoke,
"My dear father, when the night broke,

When the sky was dark and the sun did rest,
I used to come to you and sleep on your chest.

Now I know that you will be no more,
How I wish I could sleep like before."

No words could Husain say,
Upon the burning sands he lay.

Sakina rested her innocent mind
And lay there crying for quite some time.

Then she quietly from his chest arose,
Kissed him goodbye and stood near his horse.

Her eyes shed a river of tears;
She could see the glimmering swords and spears.

She watched her father mount up high,
"My dear father, goodbye . . . goodbye."

Her small hand was raised in farewell,
Her heart broken in this last farewell.

She watched her father gallop away,
No words could she speak or say.

Crying she rushed to her mother's tent,
Into her mother's outstretched arms she went.

Sobbing and quivering the child did cry,
"I don't want my father to die."

Suddenly a cry went up in the enemy ranks,
The water murmured at the river bank.

There was a quaking and trembling in the ground,
A frightening, horrible, horrendous sound.

And soon the beating of drums Sakina did hear,
And saw her father's head aloft on a spear.

Again the Masoom began to cry,
"O my father, goodbye . . . goodbye."

Then suddenly horses began to near,
She saw those glimmering swords and spears.

And all of a sudden the tents were on fire,
The baking flames rose higher and higher.

In the baking desert the camps are ablaze,
The flickering fingers of the frightening maze.

The sky is dark, smoke fills the air,
A little child runs here and there.

A weak, ill youth tries to hobble from the fire,
A boy is seen with clothes afire.

Soldiers loot these burning tents,
Confusion is amongst these flickering tents.

From amongst this is heard an innocent cry,
"My father, why have you gone? Why, O why?"

A slap is heard, the child does weep;
She is hungry, thirsty, tired, weak.

A soldier rips the earrings from her ears,
Blood mingles with her silver-like tears.

The sky is dark, there is a chill in the air,
Zainab counts all the children there.

She finds that one little child has gone,
Suddenly she feels all alone.

Sakina is that little child,
Husain's little one – so sweet and mild.

Worried, Zainab calls Umme Kulsum,
Separating they go into the darkness and gloom.

Stumbling and falling here and there,
Zainab calls the Masoom everywhere.

"Sakina, my dear come to me,
In this darkness I cannot see."

But from the darkness comes no answering call,
Zainab continues to stumble and fall.

Tears glistened on her now aged face,
Of the young Sakina she can find no trace.

Hopelessly she falls upon the ground,
From the eerie darkness there comes no sound.

Then looking in the direction of her brother's
corpse,
And looking at where he fell from his horse,

She cries, "My dear brother, Sakina I cannot find,
Lead me to her and settle my mind."

Then from behind the clouds comes the silvery
moon,
It brightens the darkness and the gloom.

Upon Hussain's body the silvery rays fall,
His sister, Zainab, he seems to call.

"Zainab, my sister come over here,
Sakina, my child, is lying here."

Zainab approaches with a silent step,
She comes to the place where a child has wept.

The child lies silent, quiet, pure,
Is she alive? Zainab is not sure.

This infant holds her dead father in an embrace,
Silver beams of light flit across her silent face.

Gently, Zainab touches the tiny head,
The child arouses from her father's chest.

She stares at her aunt with her bewildered face,
"My dear aunt, why do you come to this place?

Please, O please, let me stay,
My father sleeps – I cannot go away."

As the sky blackens like an omen of doom,
Zainab consoles the weeping Masoom.

When finally Sakina falls into the realms of sleep –
Into the gentle loving arms of peace,

Zainab picks her up with her aged back,
And carries her slowly back to camp.

But Sakina's sleep is haunted by dreams,
Sad, cruel, unforgettable dreams.

Dreams that tell her how each loved one died;
How that day she cried and cried.

How no-one from the battlefield did return,
How that day the tents did burn,

How her uncle Abbas went to the river side,
How he went to get her water from the other side,

How even he did not return,
Not even when the tents did burn.

"Sakina, Sakina," she hears someone say,
"Water has come, my child awake."

Sakina stares at Zainab with puzzled eyes,
The tears on her face have still not dried.

"O my aunt, has water really come?
Has my uncle Abbas returned?"

Her tears Zainab tries to control,
She tries to control her broken soul.

"No, my child, Abbas has not come,
Drink, my dear, water has come."

Softly, little Sakina cries,
Then looks at Zainab with innocent eyes.

"My dearest aunt, I know you thirst,
But why do you give me water first?"

At first Zainab knows not what to say,
Then she looks far away.

"Sakina, you are the youngest here,
You must be the first to drink my dear."

Suddenly Sakina runs outside,
She takes the sparkling water outside.

"Sakina, my child don't go out there,
Sakina! Sakina! Come back from there!"

But the infant girl runs on and on,
Into the darkness the child has gone.

"But you said the youngest must drink first,
My baby brother, Ali Asghar, thirsts.

I come to this place to give this to him,
This cool water for him I bring.

O my aunt, I see him not,
Where has he gone? Where has he gone?"

Zainab now has tears in her eyes.
Holding Sakina, she replies,

"Child the babe lies not here,
He lies in a place far from here.

In paradise your infant brother does sleep,
Dry your eyes – you must not weep.

Come my child, let us return,
The night will pass, it will soon be morn."

The two return from the frightening gloom,
But these words are heard on the lips of the young
Masoom.

"My uncle please return from the river shore,
I promise to ask for water no more."

And a body answers by the river side,
"Sakina, Sakina, my dearest child."

A MOTHER'S SORROW

As the sun's golden rays begin to light the sky,
A lone lady is heard to cry.

She trudges across the baking sand,
She holds a blood-drenched shirt in her hands.

A headless body lies before her feet,
Uncontrollably she begins to weep.

This was her son who was killedf yesterday,
She looks at him and begins to pray.

Her mournful cries fill the sky,
O how his life went passing by!

For three days he could drink nor eat,
Under uncontrollable heat.

Before his aged lonesome eyes,
He saw how friends and relatives died.

How a baby son was killed in his hands,
How a well-loved brother died near the river banks.

How his nephew was cut to tiny pieces,
How were orphaned little nieces.

But the lonely lady walks along,
Her lonely spirit walks on and on.

Across the blood stained golden sands,
Across the wild and lonely lands.

Crying and weeping she walks along,
Her spirit just walks on and on . . .

THE DREAM

A solitary figure stood upon the sand,
With a broken sword held in her hand.

With a proud look, and head held high,
But with a heart that longed to cry.

Often she glanced across the sand,
Across the barren and lonely land –

To a headless body, a part of her own,
By whose side she had grown.

To a tiny grave that near broke her heart,
To a strewn body, torn apart.

And often she glanced at the river side,
Where her dear brother Abbas, had died.

And often she'd look far away
To where her father Ali's grave lay.

Suddenly she saw a cloud of sand –
She clutched the sword tight in her hand.

A rider from Najaf began to near,
She was bold and had no fear.

Boldly she stepped forward and said,
"Leave us O stranger, our family is dead."

But the stranger came nearer and nearer still,
With fiery anger Zainab was filled,

"O stranger do not torment us more,
There is still more torture for us in store,

Our situation do you not see?
Go O stranger! Listen to me!"

But the stranger approached at a galloping pace,
And lifted the veil away from his face.

There before her stood her father Ali,
His eyes were filled with tears she could see.

"Zainab, to protect you I have come,
Zainab my child what have they done?"

But Zainab. her grief, could no longer control,
She told of her pains with heart and soul.

"O father look how late you have come,
Look at the evil that has been done.

Where were you when Qasim died?
When Abbas was killed by the river side?

Ahen Ali Asghar's neck was pierced by an arrow.
When our hearts were filled with total sorrow,

When Sakina's ear-rings were ripped from her ears,
When she cried out with streaming tears.

When Husain's head was raised on a spear,
O my father, did you not hear?

Did you not see
Our burning tents, our call for plea?

When our tents were burnt by Yazid's forces,
When friends were crushed under the hooves of
horses.

O my father now you come,
Look the evil has been done."

She was weeping and sobbing in every part,
As she told the story of her sad heart.

When she raised her head from the ground,
She could hear not a single sound.

She knew she was once more all alone,
She rose to her feet without a groan.

She cleared her eyes so she could see,
Raised her head and cried 'Ya Ali'.